T0396737

Praise for *Our Singapore River*:

"Tina Sim and Alan Bay have produced another well-researched and page-turning graphic novel about the Singapore River of yesteryear. In today's dizzying world you cannot stop time, and nothing stays the same. But this new book captures and vividly reimagines the essence of this landscape and the people who inhabited it. As we delve into it we get to bask in the tumult of sights, sounds and smells of the Singapore River — a special place suffused with life, creativity and colour."

Aaron Lee, Writer-poet and co-founder of the
Laniakea Culture Collective, an intercultural art practice

"What to expect from this book!
✓ Beautiful illustrations
✓ Captivating storyline
✓ Historic knowledge
X Infamous river stench

Tina and Alan have woven a magical tale of the Singapore River, Past and Present. This book is such a joy to read!"

Isaac (11) and Nathan (8) Quah

"The book tells the history of the Singapore River, which is very interesting. There was a cool lost island called Pulau Saigon. The river used to be very dirty, but you could swim in it! This book showed me that many immigrants passed through the Singapore River and that it holds a lot of stories and legends. I enjoyed learning about the Singapore River through these stories."

Renee Lai (9)

Published by

WS Education, an imprint of
World Scientific Publishing Co. Pte. Ltd.
5 Toh Tuck Link, Singapore 596224
USA office: 27 Warren Street, Suite 401-402, Hackensack, NJ 07601
UK office: 57 Shelton Street, Covent Garden, London WC2H 9HE

National Library Board, Singapore Cataloguing in Publication Data
Name(s): Sim, Tina Soek Tien, 1966– | Bay, Alan, illustrator.
Title: Our Singapore River / by Tina Sim ; illustrated by Alan Bay.
Other Title(s): Time travel, Singapore!
Description: Singapore : WS Education, [2023] | Includes bibliography.
Identifier(s): ISBN 978-981-12-5904-3 (hardback) | 978-981-12-6015-5 (paperback)
Subject(s): LCSH: Singapore--Social conditions--History. |
    Singapore--Economic conditions--History. |
    Singapore River (Singapore)--Economic aspects--History.
Classification: DDC 959.57--dc23

British Library Cataloguing-in-Publication Data
A catalogue record for this book is available from the British Library.

Supported by

The views expressed here are solely those of the author
in her private capacity and do not in any way represent
the views of the National Heritage Board and/or any
government agencies.

Design: Alan Bay
Desk Editor: Daniele Lee

Printed in Singapore

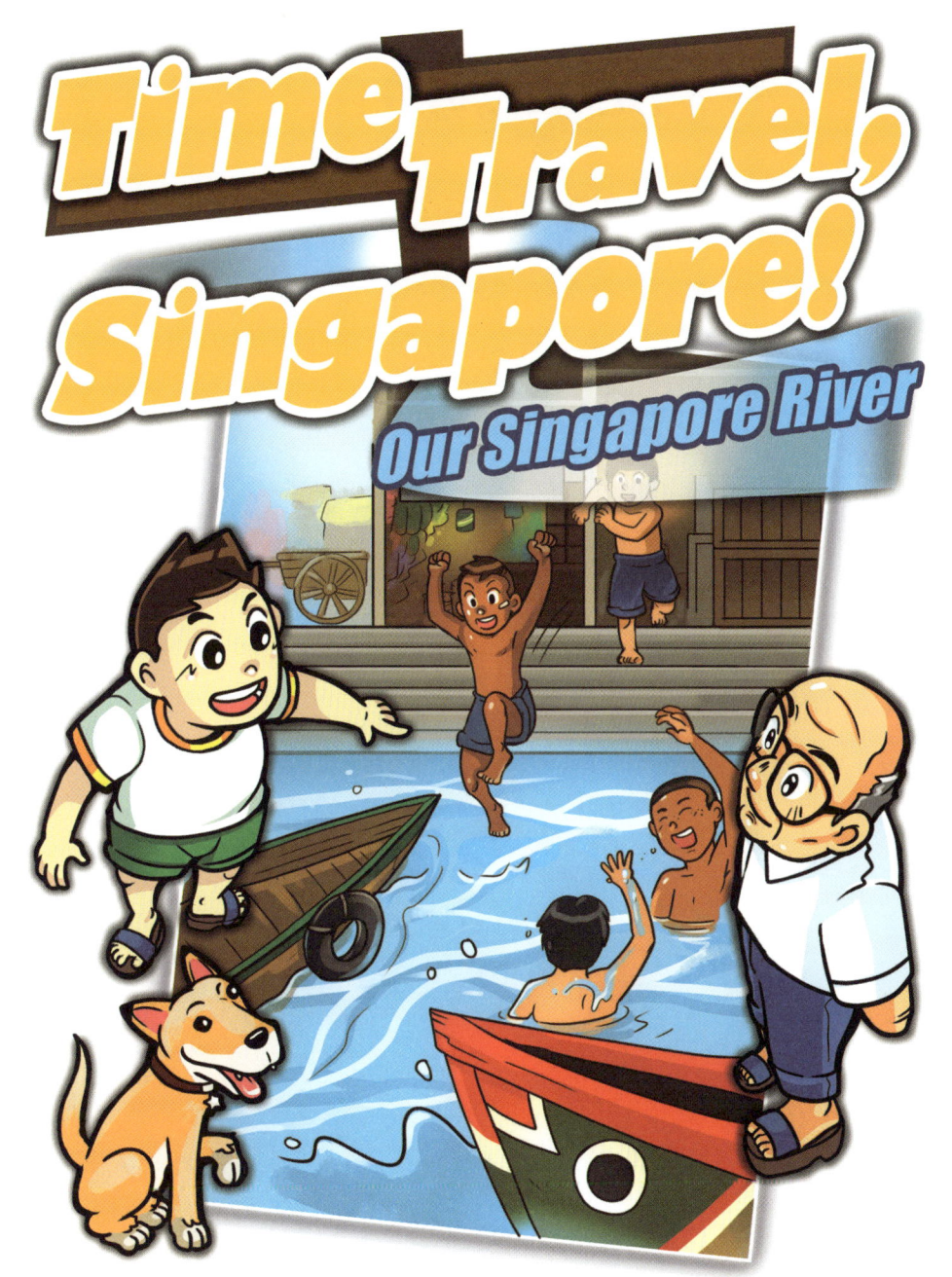

Time Travel, Singapore!

Our Singapore River

Tina Sim   Illustrated by Alan Bay

WS Education

NEW JERSEY · LONDON · SINGAPORE · BEIJING · SHANGHAI · HONG KONG · TAIPEI · CHENNAI · TOKYO

CONTENTS

THE SINGAPORE RIVER

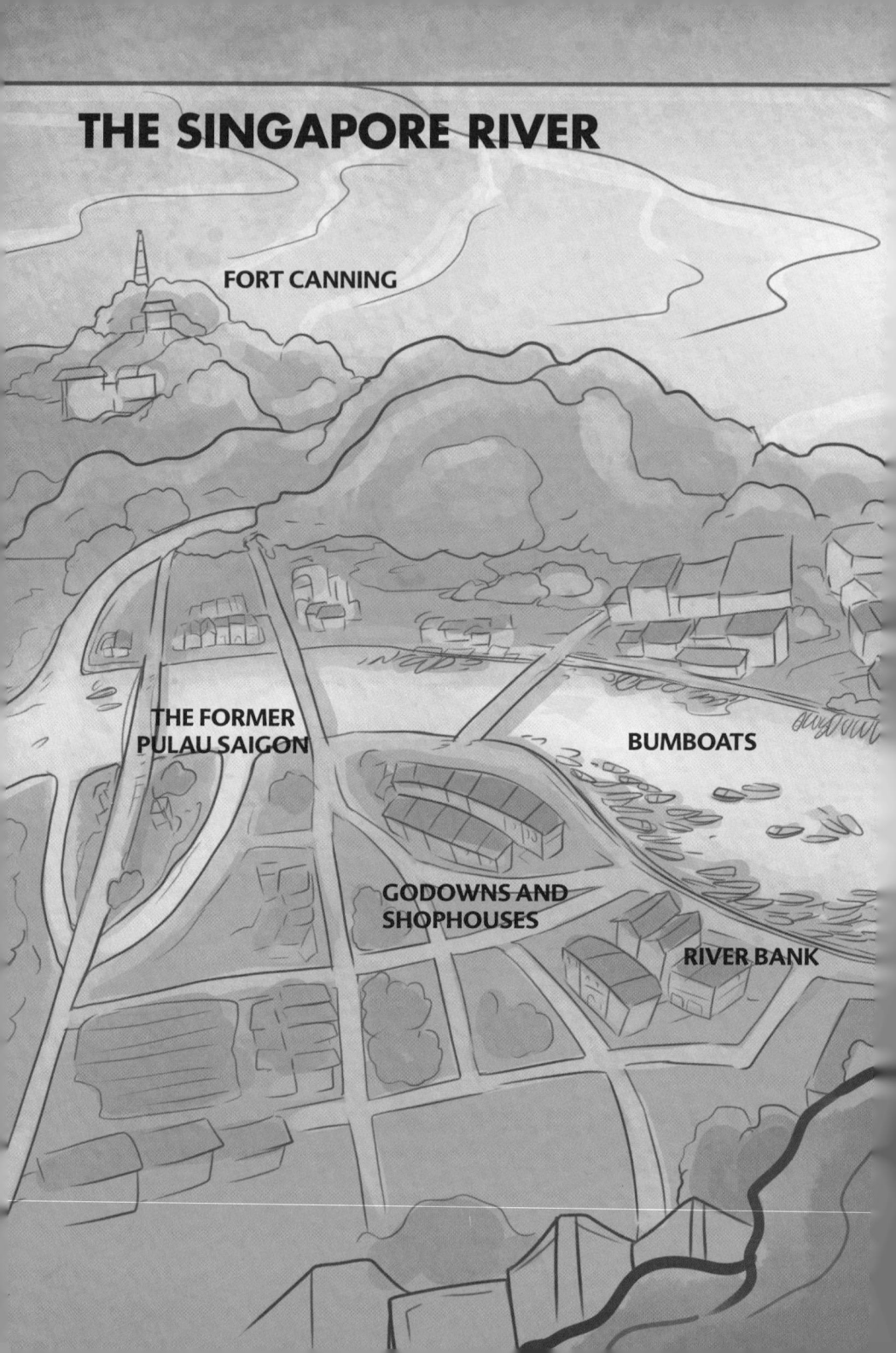

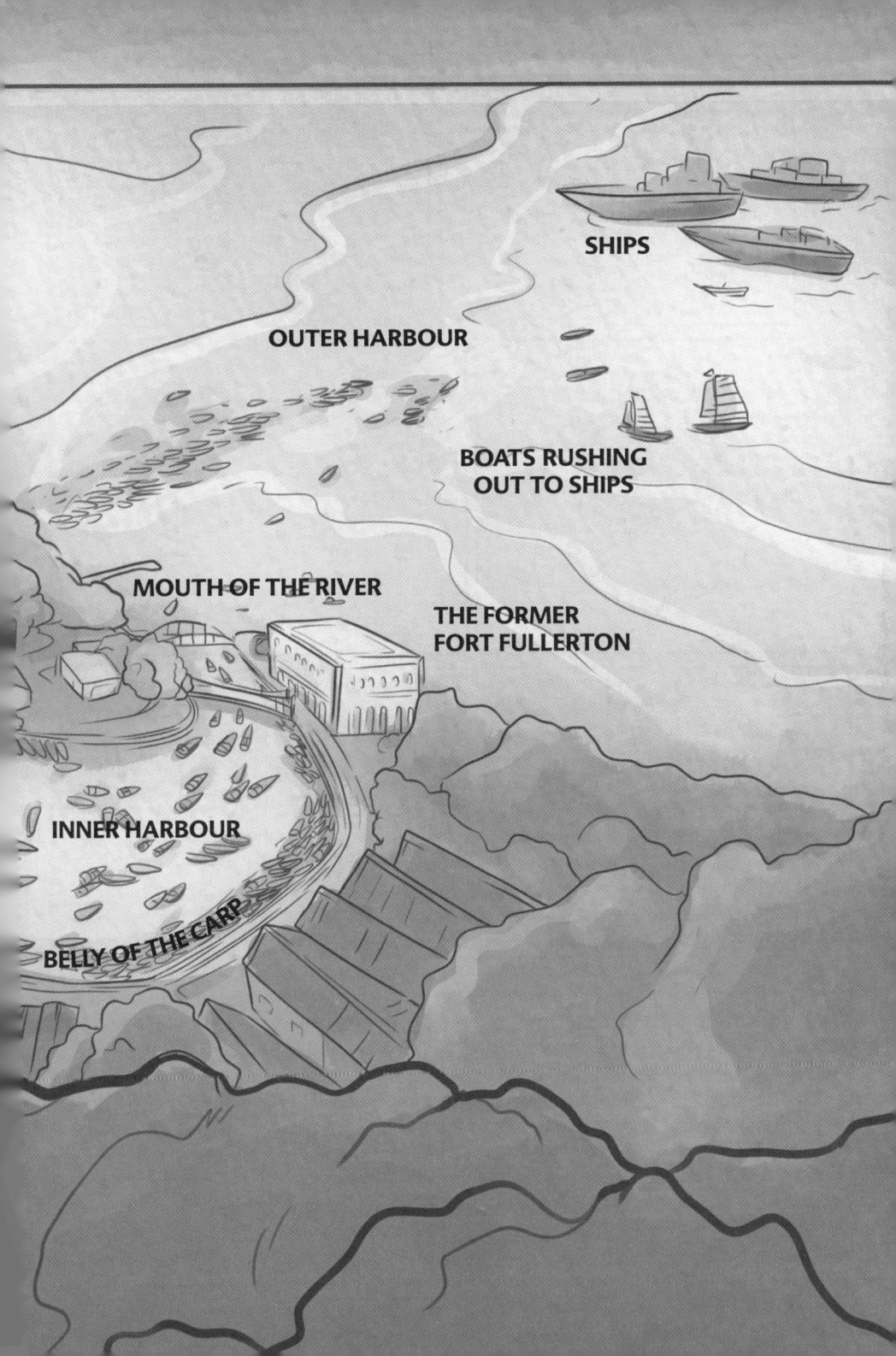

CHAPTER 1 A VISIT TO THE RIVER

IT'S JUST WATER AND SAND...

DO YOU KNOW GRANDPA USED TO LIVE BY THE RIVER?

I USED TO DO THIS.

SHALL WE?

SPLASH!

WHERE ARE WE?

AT THE SINGAPORE RIVER... WHEN I WAS A YOUNG BOY.

SINGAPORE RIVER WAS "COLOURFUL" IN THE PAST.

DURING LOW TIDE WHEN IT WAS SHALLOW, THE RIVER WAS BLACK LIKE *KOPI-O** AND HAD A FOUL SMELL.

* BLACK COFFEE

WHEN IT RAINED, THE RIVER BECAME BROWNISH LIKE *TEH-C***.

** TEA WITH MILK

BUT DURING HIGH TIDE, THE WATER WAS ADORABLE LIKE GREEN TEA, AND WITHOUT MUCH RUBBISH! THAT WAS OUR FAVOURITE TIME TO DIVE INTO THE RIVER!

DO WE THINK WE CAN WALK ON THE RUBBISH FROM THIS END TO THE OTHER?

WE ALWAYS KEPT OUR HEADS ABOVE WATER...

AND NEVER SWALLOW!

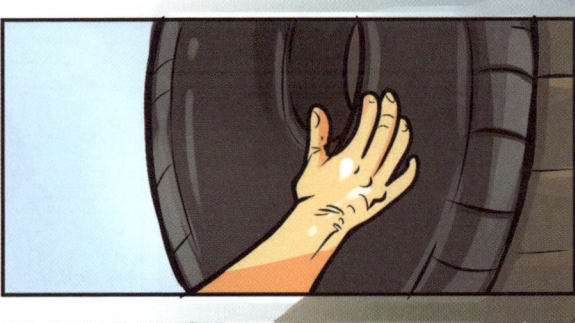

COME ON!

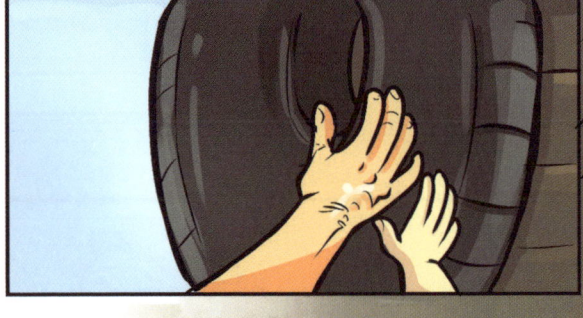

LET GO. WE STOP HERE.

WHY? THIS IS FUN. I WANT TO KEEP GOING.

WHY ARE WE GETTING OUT?

IT IS TOO DANGEROUS. WE HAVE TO STAY HERE IN THE RIVER.

BUT WHERE IS THE BOAT GOING?

IT'S GOING OUT TO THE SEA, TO BRING IN THE CARGO FROM THE BIG SHIPS.

WHY CAN'T THE BIG SHIPS COME IN THEMSELVES?

CHAPTER 2   THE RIVER AND THE SEA

THE SHIPS HAVE TO STAY OUTSIDE IN THE OPEN SEA, AS THEY ARE TOO BIG TO FIT ON THE RIVER. ONLY THE SMALL BOATS CAN ENTER THE RIVER, WHICH IS SHALLOW. THE MOUTH OF THE RIVER IS ALSO TOO NARROW FOR THEM TO BE ABLE TO FIT THROUGH.

WE USED TO CALL THEM OUTER HARBOUR AND INNER HARBOUR.

THIS SKYLINE IS SO ICONIC IT WAS OFTEN USED ON POSTCARDS FEATURING OLD SINGAPORE.

DHOWS FROM ARABIA AND INDIA

CLIPPERS FROM THE WEST

GOLEKKAN FROM THE INDONESIAN ARCHIPELAGO

PALARI FROM THE INDONESIAN ARCHIPELAGO

WANGKANG FROM INDO-CHINA

LETEH-LETEH FROM THE INDONESIAN ARCHIPELAGO

PADEWAKANG FROM THE INDONESIAN ARCHIPELAGO

PINAS FROM THE MALAY PENINSULA

TONGKANG

WE EVEN MADE OUR OWN BOATS – TONGKANG AND TWAKOW!

TWAKOW

SO MANY SHIPS FROM SO MANY COUNTRIES!

JUNKS FROM CHINA

31

CHAPTER 3 GOING OUT TO SEA

THEY ARE DONE UNLOADING. THEY ARE COMING BACK INTO THE RIVER.

CAN I TRY?

IT'S VERY HARD WORK, GRANDPA.

YOU USED TO DO THIS TOO, RIGHT?

YES, THANKFULLY THE BOATS WERE MOTORISED LATER ON.

CHAPTER 5   A BOATMAN'S WORK

WE ALSO HAVE TO PACK SUCH THAT THE BOAT CAN STILL BE STABLE. IF THE BOAT TIPS, EVERYTHING FALLS INTO THE WATER, ESPECIALLY IF THERE IS A SUDDEN WIND OR TIDE.

IN 1917, THERE WAS AN EARLY MORNING SQUALL. IT CAUGHT US ALL BY SURPRISE. FIFTY BOATS SANK THAT DAY. THEY WERE CARRYING RICE, SUGAR AND DRIED FISH. IT ALL DISAPPEARED INTO THE BOTTOM OF THE SEA.

DUCK!

THAT WAS FUN!

IT'S NOT SO FUN IF YOU GET STUCK. IF THE TIDE IS HIGH AND OUR CARGO IS STACKED TOO HIGH, WE CAN'T PASS UNDER THE BRIDGE.

WHY ARE THEY POURING WATER INTO THE BOAT?

TO LOWER THE BOAT SO IT IS LOW ENOUGH TO PASS UNDER THE BRIDGE.

WON'T IT DAMAGE THE CARGO?

SOMETIMES WE CAN'T WAIT TILL LOW TIDE.

AH, BUT THE BIG SHIPS MIGHT NOT EVEN BE ABLE TO PASS THROUGH DURING LOW TIDE, BECAUSE THEY ARE TOO TALL!

SOMETIMES, THE BOATS HAVE TO WAIT TILL LOW TIDE BEFORE THEY COULD PASS UNDER CAVENAGH BRIDGE.

WHAT HAPPENS WHEN IT RAINS?

WE COVER THE GOODS WITH A RUBBER SHEET.

THE CARGO IS VERY PRECIOUS. IT'S WORTH A LOT OF MONEY. WE TAKE VERY GOOD CARE OF IT. SOMETIMES WE SLEEP ON BOARD TO GUARD IT.

YOU MEAN YOU SLEEP ON THIS BOAT? WHERE?

WE MAKE DO. WE SAVE ALL THE SPACE WE CAN FOR THE CARGO.

AFTER SLEEPING ON A BOAT, I LEARNT TO SLEEP ANYWHERE.

YOU STILL DO!

Z Z Z

ACTUALLY, I MISS THE ROCKING OF THE BOAT WITH THE WAVES AND THE SOUNDS OF THE RIVER.

YOU DON'T GO HOME?

WE ARE USUALLY ON STANDBY, SO WE CAN HEAD OUT IMMEDIATELY WHEN THE SHIPS ARRIVE. WE TRY TO BE THE FIRST BOAT OUT, SO, MANY OF US LIVE ON THE BOATS.

SOME LIVE UNDER THE BRIDGES OR BY THE RIVERSIDE. SO WE CAN GET TO OUR BOATS QUICKLY WHEN THE SHIPS COME IN.

HOW DO YOU GO TO THE TOILET?

GUESS!

WHY IS EVERYONE RUSHING OUT?

SO WE CAN BE THE FIRST TO REACH THE BIG SHIPS WHEN THEY ARRIVE. HAVEN'T YOU HEARD OF THE PHRASE "THE EARLY BIRD CATCHES THE WORM"?

AH! THE EARLY BOAT... CATCHES THE SHIP!

CHAPTER 6   A VERY BUSY RIVER

I SPY RED EYES.

THIS PARTICULAR BUMBOAT IS CALLED A *TWAKOW*. THOSE WITH RED EYES MEANS ITS OWNER IS TEOCHEW*.

I SPY GREEN AND RED EYES.

THOSE WITH GREEN AND RED PAINTED AROUND THE EYES BELONG TO THE HOKKIENS*.

*THE TEOCHEWS AND HOKKIENS ARE DIALECT GROUPS FROM DIFFERENT REGIONS OF SOUTH CHINA.

WHAT ARE THE EYES FOR?

THE EYES ENABLE THE BOATS TO SEE DANGERS AHEAD, LIKE UNDERWATER ROCKS.

WOW! LIKE SUPERMAN WITH X-RAY VISION!

THEY ALSO WARD OFF EVIL SPIRITS.

THERE'S ANOTHER REASON. THEY SHOW US IF WE ARE OVERLOADED. THE EYES MUST ALWAYS BE ABOVE WATER.

SO MANY CLEVER TRICKS.

I SPY TYRES.

WHAT ARE THEY USED FOR?

BESIDES BEING FOR US TO HANG ON TO?

BUMP!!

SHOCK ABSORBERS. HOW CLEVER!

I KNOW THAT GRIN. WHAT ARE YOU UP TO?

SC363A

SC 491K

I SPY NUMBERS...

EVEN THE SMALL BOATS HAVE NUMBERS!

ALL BOATS GOING UP AND DOWN THE RIVER HAVE TO BE REGISTERED. YOU CAN'T ENTER THE RIVER IF YOU DON'T HAVE A NUMBER.

THE RIVER HAS ITS OWN LAWS. THERE IS A LIMIT ON THE AMOUNT OF TIME THE BOATS CAN STAY IN THE PARKING LOT. THE BIGGER BOATS CAN ONLY PARK PARALLEL TO THE RIVER BANK, AND THEN NO MORE THAN THREE SIDE BY SIDE.

LET ME COUNT.

CAN YOU ALSO SEE THE FLOATING TANKS IN THE MIDDLE OF THE RIVER?

THE BOATS HAVE TO BE PARKED INSIDE THEIR LINE. YOU WOULD GET A TICKET FROM THE RIVER POLICE OTHERWISE.

THE RIVER IS VERY ORGANISED. MUM WOULD LIKE IT HERE.

TRAFFIC JAM.

TRAFFIC JAM. PARKING PLACES. LANES. RULES. TRAFFIC FINES.

THE RIVER IS LIKE A ROAD. AND THE BOATS ARE THE CARS CARRYING PEOPLE TO AND FRO.

WHAT ARE THOSE BOYS DOING?

IN PLACES WHERE THERE ARE NO BRIDGES, PEOPLE ARE FERRIED ACROSS BY BOATS.

HEY GRANDPA, IF WE STAY, I CAN DO THAT TOO.

YOU WILL REALLY LIKE IT. THEY LIVE ON THE RIVER TOO.

LUCKY WOULD HAVE FRIENDS HERE TOO!

THE RIVER IS FULL OF LIFE!

CHAPTER 7 A COOLIE'S WORK

THAT'S WHAT THE STEPS ARE FOR!

IT LOOKS LIKE THE SACK WEIGHS MORE THAN HIM.

EACH SACK CAN BE OVER 100KG.

THAT'S THE WEIGHT OF YOU AND ME COMBINED.

68

THAT LOOKS PAINFUL!

HE IS CARRYING EACH FISH ONE BY ONE!

THE COOLIES ARE LIKE ACROBATS!
THEY ARE SO AGILE!

CAN I TRY?

good morning 안녕 早上好

WOOBLE

ERR... MAYBE NOT.

FOLLOW ME.

YOU'VE STILL GOT IT!

YOU HAVE TO BOUNCE WITH THE PLANK. ONCE YOU GET THE RHYTHM, IT'S EASIER. AND YOUR LEGS WILL HURT LESS AT NIGHT.

GRANDPA, YOU'RE LIKE A SUPERHERO. IT'S LIKE YOU PUT ON YOUR CAPE AND YOU'RE OFF TO DO ALL THESE SUPERHERO THINGS.

HERE'S YOUR CAPE, GRANDPA.

GRANDPA MUST HAVE BEEN REALLY COOL WHEN HE WAS YOUNG!

CHAPTER 8 INTO THE WAREHOUSES

WHAT IS THAT MAN DOING?

HE IS CHECKING THE QUALITY OF THE RICE.

HE SAYS THE RICE IS OF GOOD QUALITY.

THE COOLIES CAN NOW TAKE THE RICE INTO THE GODOWN.

GODOWN?

A WAREHOUSE. THE GOODS WILL STAY IN THE GODOWNS UNTIL THE SHIP THAT WILL TAKE THE CARGO TO ITS NEW DESTINATION COMES INTO PORT.

WHY DO THEY CALL THEM GODOWNS? WHY NOT GO-UPS?

IS IT TIME FOR LUNCH?

WE COLLECT ONE FOR EACH SACK WE BRING IN. AT THE END OF THE DAY, THEY ARE COUNTED. WE ARE PAID BY HOW MANY WE COLLECT.

GROAN

WHAT'S THE CHOPSTICK FOR?

THAT'S SO CLEVER.

MOST OF THESE GODOWNS KEEP A COUPLE OF PYTHONS AROUND TO GET RID OF THE RATS.

I WANT TO SEE A PYTHON TOO.

LUCKY HAS ALL THE FUN!

CHAPTER 9   A DAY ON THE RIVER

WHAT IS HAPPENING?

A SHIP HAS JUST COME IN.

THESE BOATS ARE GOING OUT TO THE BIG SHIPS IN THE BIG HARBOUR TO BRING THE CARGO IN.

THAT'S WHY ONLY THE EMPTY BOATS ARE GOING OUT?

HOW DO THEY KNOW? THE SEA IS SO FAR AWAY.

SEE THAT TALL HILL? THAT'S FORT CANNING.

CAN YOU SEE THE FLAGSTAFF?

YES. IT HAS MANY DIFFERENT FLAGS WITH DIFFERENT DESIGNS AND COLOURS!

THE FLAGS HAVE A VERY IMPORTANT FUNCTION. THEY SHOW WHERE THE SHIPS COME FROM, WHERE THEY ARE GOING, AND THE TYPE OF CARGO THEY CARRY.

YOU MEAN THE FLAGS ARE LIKE MESSAGES?

YES. THEY CAN EVEN SIGNAL IF THERE IS AN INFECTIOUS DISEASE, SUCH AS SMALLPOX, ON BOARD.

THAT'S SO CLEVER. TO USE A TALL FLAGSTAFF ON A TALL HILL...

YES, FORT CANNING PROVIDES A STRATEGIC VIEW OF THE RIVER AND THE HARBOUR. ANY SIGNAL SENT FROM THE HILL CAN BE SEEN CLEARLY BY ALL.

IF THERE WERE A FIRE IN TOWN, A FLAG WOULD ALSO BE FLOWN TO ALERT PEOPLE.

AFTER SUCH A LONG JOURNEY, THE SHIPS WILL NEED FRESH FOOD AND WATER. THESE SAMPANS BRING FOOD AND WATER TO THEM.

THE SAILORS WILL ALSO WANT TO COME TO SHORE. THESE SAMPANS WILL FERRY THEM IN.

WHAT ABOUT THOSE LITTLE BOATS? THEY ARE TOO SMALL TO CARRY MUCH CARGO.

... START OF THE JUNK SEASON...

... THE SATIN FROM THE LAST SHIP FETCHED AN EXCELLENT PRICE FROM THE EUROPEANS...

I CAN FIND OUT IF MY FAMILY RECEIVED THE MONEY I SENT BY THE LAST SHIP.

NOW YOU WILL KNOW IF YOUR WIFE GAVE BIRTH TO A SON OR DAUGHTER.

THE WORKERS ARE EXCITED BECAUSE THE SHIPS BRING MAIL FROM THEIR FAMILIES BACK HOME.

THAT'S RICE. THAT'S FISH. THAT'S RATTAN.

THAT'S...

GOODS FROM CHINA:
SILK, PORCELAIN, LACQUERWARE, TEA, RICE, EARTHERNWARE, TILES, GRANITE SLABS, PAPER UMBRELLAS, VERMICELLI, DRIED FRUIT, JOSS STICKS AND JOSS PAPER, SILKS, SATINS, CAMPHOR, CAMLET, NANKEENS, SUGAR CANDY, MEDICINES, TWINE, FLOUR, CRACKERS, PAINT AND COMBS.

GOODS FROM OTHER PARTS OF ASIA, LIKE THAILAND AND VIETNAM:
SUGAR, SALT, RICE, COCONUT OIL, CAST IRON, CULINARY UTENSILS, STICKLAC, RAW SILK, TONKIN LEAD, PICKLED PORK, HOGS, LARD AND LIVESTOCK.

GOODS FROM BRITAIN:
MACHINERY, IRONWORK SUCH AS ANCHORS AND GRAPNELS, BEER, CANVAS, COPPER SHEATHING, CORDAGE, COTTON TWIST, EARTHERNWARE, GOLD AND SILVER THREAD, GUNPOWDER, IRON, STEEL, LEAD, PAINT, COTTON GOODS, SPELTER, SPIRITS, SUNDRIES, GLASSWARE, WINES, WOOLLENS AND IRONWARE.

GOODS FROM THE INDIAN SUBCONTINENT:
OPIUM, WHEAT, RICE, GRAM SEED, GUNNIES, SALTPETRE, INDIGO DYE, IVORY, COTTON, SILK, SUGAR, SALT, SPICES, SAFFRON, TEA, GLASS BANGLES, STONE BEADS, MUSK OF DEER, FRANKINCENSE, MYRRH AND PRECIOUS GEMS LIKE AMETHYST, RUBIES, GARNET, SAPPHIRE AND TOPAZ.

GOODS FROM THE INDONESIAN ISLANDS: COFFEE, GOLD DUST, SAGO, TORTOISE SHELLS, TREPANG, SHARKS' FIN, BIRD'S NEST, COCONUT, COPRA, BEESWAX, EDIBLE SEAWEED, SANDALWOOD, AGARWOOD, GAMBIER, GUTTA-PERCHA, DRAGON'S BLOOD, STICKLAC, EBONY, GOLD, RATTAN, RUBBER, TIN, AND SPICES LIKE NUTMEG, CINNAMON AND PEPPER.

MUM WOULD LIKE IT HERE.

WE BECAME KNOWN AS THE "EMPORIUM OF THE EAST". IN OUR FIRST TWO YEARS AS A FREE PORT, SOME 200,000 TONS OF CARGO PASSED THROUGH THE PORT.

200,000 吨

EMPORIUM! I KNOW WHAT THAT MEANS – A PLACE THAT SELLS A LOT OF THINGS.

MANY EXOTIC ANIMALS ALSO PASSED THROUGH OUR PORT. THERE WERE PEACOCKS, BIRDS AND HAWKSBILL TURTLES.

OH, AND ELEPHANTS TOO!

WE WERE A MAJOR CENTRE FOR WILDLIFE TRADE. BIRDS WERE KEPT AS PETS OR KILLED FOR THEIR FEATHERS OR RELEASED FOR RELIGIOUS PURPOSES.

ELEPHANTS WERE NEEDED FOR ROYAL PROCESSIONS.

TIGERS AND RHINOCEROSES WERE USED FOR MEDICINAL PURPOSES.

THERE WERE OTHER ANIMALS LIKE ORANGUTANS, TAPIRS AND SLOW LEMURS.

NO FAIR, GRANDPA, YOUR LIFE WAS SO EXCITING!

THEY'VE FINISHED UNLOADING! COME, LUCKY!

IT IS HUUUUUUUGE!

WOOF! WOOF~ WOOF~

WHY, GRANDPA?

WHY WHAT?

WHY DO ALL THE CARGO COME HERE?

BECAUSE OF THE WINDS...

IN THE DAYS BEFORE WE HAD MOTORS, SHIPS HARNESSED THE WIND TO TRAVEL.

THEY RELIED ON SEASONAL WINDS CALLED MONSOONS. MONSOON WINDS BLOW IN DIFFERENT DIRECTIONS AT DIFFERENT TIMES OF THE YEAR.

A SHIP WOULD SET SAIL IN ONE DIRECTION AT THE BEGINNING OF THE YEAR AND COME HOME LATER IN THE YEAR WHEN THE WIND REVERSES DIRECTION.

OH, LIKE MAKING A U-TURN!

HOW CLEVER! THEY LET THE WIND BLOW THEM BACK HOME!

LIKE ME TAKING A BUS OUT TO SCHOOL WHEN IT TRAVELS IN ONE DIRECTION. AND AFTER SCHOOL, TAKING THE BUS IN THE OPPOSITE DIRECTION TO COME HOME.

WHEN THE NORTHEAST MONSOON BLOWS, THE SHIPS WILL SAIL FROM CHINA. WHEN THEY GET HERE, THEY TRADE WITH THE MERCHANTS HERE, AND LEAVE THEIR CARGO OF SILK, RICE AND CAMPHOR IN THE GODOWNS. THEN, WHEN THE MONSOON REVERSES DIRECTION AND BLOWS IN THE OPPOSITE SOUTHWEST DIRECTION, THE SHIPS WILL HARNESS THE WIND AND SAIL BACK TO CHINA.

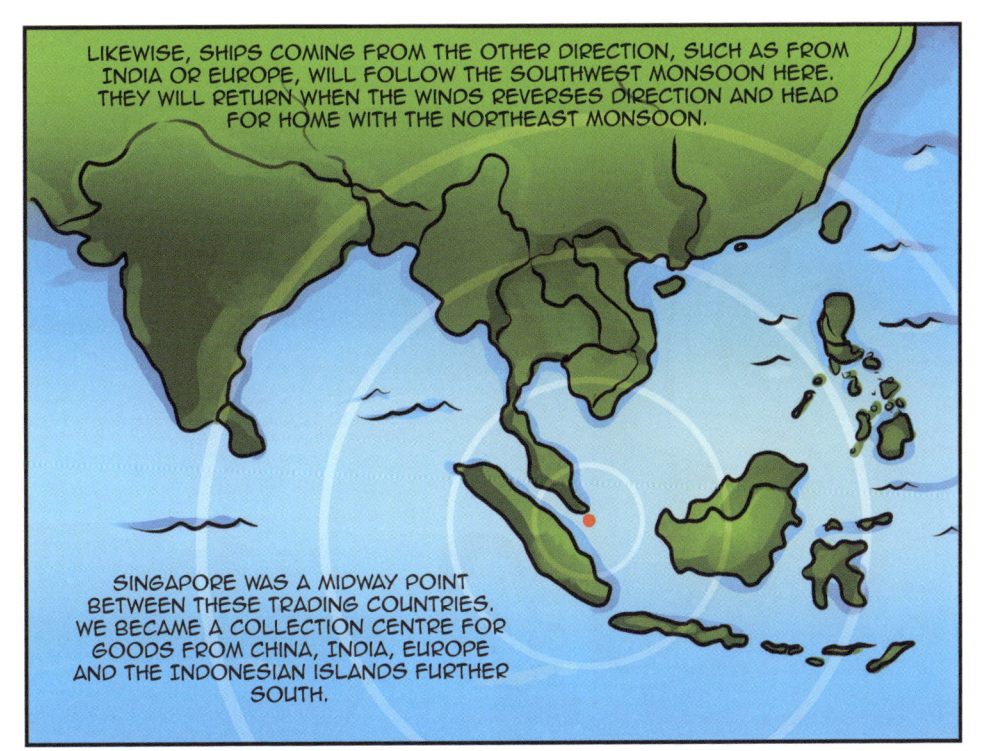

LIKEWISE, SHIPS COMING FROM THE OTHER DIRECTION, SUCH AS FROM INDIA OR EUROPE, WILL FOLLOW THE SOUTHWEST MONSOON HERE. THEY WILL RETURN WHEN THE WINDS REVERSES DIRECTION AND HEAD FOR HOME WITH THE NORTHEAST MONSOON.

SINGAPORE WAS A MIDWAY POINT BETWEEN THESE TRADING COUNTRIES. WE BECAME A COLLECTION CENTRE FOR GOODS FROM CHINA, INDIA, EUROPE AND THE INDONESIAN ISLANDS FURTHER SOUTH.

CAN WE EAT SO MUCH RICE AND FISH? AND DO WE NEED TO USE SO MANY PLATES? AND WEAR SO MUCH SILK?

WE DON'T EAT ALL THE RICE OR USE EVERYTHING THAT COMES THROUGH THE PORT! IN FACT, THE CARGO IS NOT UNPACKED AT ALL. WE ARE A SPECIAL KIND OF PORT — CALLED AN ENTREPÔT.

THE CARGO IS JUST STORED HERE. WHEN THE SHIPS OF THEIR DESTINATION ARRIVE, THE CARGO IS TAKEN OUT TO SEA AGAIN, TO BE PUT ON THE BIG SHIPS AND TAKEN TO OTHER COUNTRIES.

SO IT ENTERS AND THEN EXITS?

YES.

THEN WHY CALL IT AN "ENTERPORT"? SHOULDN'T IT BE CALLED AN "ENTER AND EXIT PORT"?

IT'S E–N–T–R–E–P–Ô–T.

ENTREPÔT REFERS TO A PORT, CITY OR WAREHOUSE WHERE GOODS ARE IMPORTED TO BE STORED OR TRADED FOR RE-EXPORT. IT IS DERIVED FROM THE FRENCH WORDS "ENTRE" MEANING "BETWEEN", AND "POSER" MEANING "PLACE".

BUT WHY HERE? HOW ABOUT ALL THE OTHER PLACES AROUND HERE?

WE HAVE A DEEP SEA HARBOUR WHERE SHIPS CAN ANCHOR WHILE THE RIVER'S CALM WATERS PROVIDE A SAFE PLACE FOR THE CARGO. THERE IS ALSO A READY SUPPLY OF FRESH WATER AND FOOD, SO SHIPS CAN REFUEL AND GET FRESH SUPPLIES.

MOST IMPORTANTLY, WE ARE A FREE PORT.

FREE?

SHIPS CAN BRING THEIR CARGO IN AND OUT OF THE PORT WITHOUT PAYING TAX ON IT. THIS MAKES THE PORT VERY ATTRACTIVE AND MANY SHIPS AND MERCHANTS COME.

CHAPTER 11 THE BELLY OF THE CARP

THERE WAS ANOTHER REASON. YOU WILL LIKE IT.

THE RIVER IS A FISH WITH A FAT STOMACH.

WELL, THE RIVER LOOKS LIKE A FISH WITH A FAT STOMACH.

IT WAS A VERY LUCKY SIGN. THE CHINESE CALLED THE RIVER THE "BELLY OF THE CARP". TO THE CHINESE, THE CARP HAS ALWAYS BEEN A SYMBOL OF GOOD FORTUNE.
THE WORD FOR FISH "YU" SOUNDS THE SAME AS THE WORDS FOR WEALTH AND PLENTY. SO THE CARP WAS SEEN AS A VERY, VERY LUCKY FISH.

DAD IS ALSO A LUCKY SYMBOL!

IS THAT WHY WE SEE SO MANY PAINTINGS OF CARP? ON PLATES, BOWLS, VASES AND PAINTINGS?

BECAUSE THE CARP HAS A LONG LIFESPAN, IT IS ALSO A SYMBOL OF LONGEVITY.

IT SWIMS VERY FAST AND IS VERY LIVELY, WHICH REPRESENTS ZEST FOR LIFE, ENERGY AND VITALITY.

WOW! THE CARP IS A FANTASTIC FISH!

I KNOW ANOTHER GOOD REASON. THE FAT BELLY MAKES IT LOOK LIKE IT'S GOING TO HAVE LOTS OF BABIES. THAT'S GOOD, RIGHT, HAVING LOTS OF BABIES?

SO, BECAUSE OF THE CARP, THE CHINESE MERCHANTS WERE ATTRACTED BY THE GOOD FENG SHUI OF THE RIVER.

IT'S SO BRIGHT.

THEY ALSO SAY THAT THE BOATS ON THE RIVER LOOK LIKE THE GLITTERY SCALES OF THE DRAGON, SO THE RIVER IS DOUBLY AUSPICIOUS.

WOAH. YOUR STORIES ARE GETTING BETTER. CARP AND DRAGON...

FENG SHUI PRACTITIONERS SEE CAVENAGH BRIDGE AT THE MOUTH OF THE RIVER AS THE DRAGON GATE. THE BUMBOATS HAVE TO FIGHT CURRENTS AND OTHER OBSTACLES TO GET TO THE MOUTH OF THE RIVER. SO, WHEN THEY SAIL SUCCESSFULLY UNDER THE CAVENAGH BRIDGE AND REACH THE SEA, THEY TOO ARE TRANSFORMED INTO MIGHTY DRAGONS.

THE BOATMEN HAD TO FIND WAYS TO PASS UNDER THE BRIDGE DURING HIGH TIDE. ONE WAY WAS TO FLOOD THE BOAT TO MAKE IT SINK LOWER!

ANOTHER CLEVER TRICK!

YOU ALL CAME UP WITH SO MANY CLEVER TRICKS! YOU WERE CARPS WHO TURNED INTO DRAGONS TOO!

THE RIVER ALSO REMINDED US OF HOME.

RONGJIANG RIVER AT MY HOMETOWN IN SWATOW, CHINA ALSO LOOKED LIKE THE "BELLY OF THE CARP". TO THE TEOCHEW PIONEERS FROM SWATOW, IT FELT LIKE HOME.

GRANDPA, WHERE DID YOU... WE COME FROM?

WE ARE TEOCHEWS, FROM SWATOW.

IT WAS NOT SO LONELY BECAUSE IT FELT LIKE HOME?

WILL YOU TAKE ME BACK TO LOOK AT IT ONE DAY?

OF COURSE!

SO THE IMMIGRANTS LIKED IT HERE. THE RIVER LOOKED LIKE HOME. THEY SET UP TRADING OFFICES AND GODOWNS HERE, IN THE BELLY WHERE GOOD FORTUNE RESIDES.

IS THAT WHY MOST OF THE TALL BUILDINGS ARE ON THE BELLY SIDE OF THE RIVER? THE FATTER THE STOMACH, THE LUCKIER IT IS?

GOOD EYE, BOY. YES. THE BELLY PART, WHICH WE KNOW NOW AS BOAT QUAY, WAS THE BUSIEST PART OF THE RIVER. MANY SHOPHOUSES WERE CROWDED INTO THIS AREA.

EVEN IN MODERN SINGAPORE, MOST OF THE SKYSCRAPERS ARE ON THE BELLY SIDE OF THE RIVER.

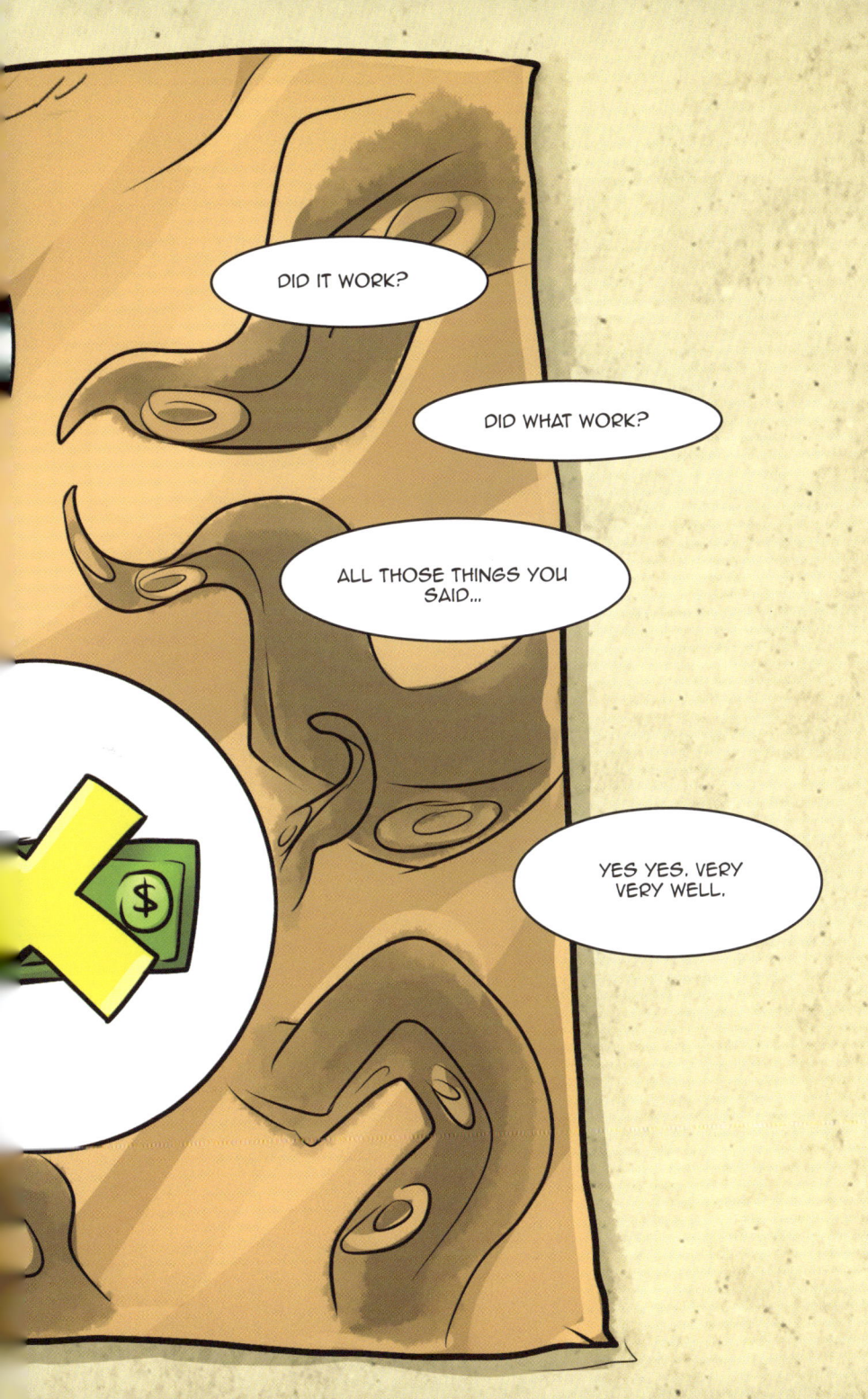

THE SHIPS AND MERCHANTS CAME. IN THE FIRST TWO YEARS AFTER IT WAS ESTABLISHED AS A FREE PORT, ALMOST 3,000 VESSELS CARRYING 200,000 TONNES OF CARGO PASSED THROUGH THE PORT.

THE RIVER WAS SO BUSY, IT LOOKED LIKE A CARPET OF BOATS. IN ITS HEYDAY, THERE WERE MORE THAN 3,000 BOATS GOING UP AND DOWN THE RIVER.

THE RIVER ALSO ATTRACTED PEOPLE HOPING TO MAKE THEIR FORTUNE. THEY CAME FROM CHINA, INDIA, THE NEIGHBOURING ISLANDS, AND FROM FARAWAY COUNTRIES LIKE EUROPE AND THE MIDDLE EAST.

THE BANKS OF THE RIVER BECAME MORE CROWDED AS MORE OFFICES, SHOPHOUSES AND GODOWNS WERE BUILT.

THE TOWN EXPANDED BEYOND THE AREAS AROUND THE RIVER. SINGAPORE AS A COUNTRY GREW FROM THE RIVER.

THE ADVENTURES OF BADANG AND THE SINGAPORE STONE

THERE WAS ONCE A SLAVE NAMED BADANG. HE SET TRAPS IN THE RIVER TO CATCH FISH.

THE NETS KEPT COMING UP EMPTY.

A HANTU* HAD BEEN STEALING HIS FISH!

*GHOST

PLEASE DON'T KILL ME. I WILL GIVE YOU ANYTHING YOU ASK FOR.

GIVE ME GREAT STRENGTH. SO GREAT I CAN UPROOT TREES WITH ONE HAND.

OKAY... BUT YOU MUST EAT MY VOMIT.

IMPRESSED WITH HIS ENORMOUS STRENGTH, THE RAJAH* MADE BADANG A COURT WARRIOR.

*KING

THE RAJAH'S MEN BUILT HIM A NEW BOAT. HE ORDERED THEM TO LAUNCH IT.

FIRST FIFTY MEN...

THEN TWO OR THREE HUNDRED... THEN TWO OR THREE THOUSAND...

BUT THEY COULD NOT MOVE THE BOAT.

THE RAJAH ORDERED BADANG TO TRY.

WITH ONE PUSH, BADANG SENT THE BOAT TO THE OTHER END OF THE RIVER!

OTHER RAJAHS HEARD OF BADANG'S FAME. THEY SENT THEIR WARRIORS TO CHALLENGE HIM.

THE RAJAH OF KLING* SENT HIS CHAMPION, WITH SEVEN SHIPS FILLED WITH TREASURES FOR THE WINNER. IF BADANG LOST, HE WOULD HAVE TO ALSO GIVE THE CHAMPION SEVEN SHIPS OF TREASURES.

*FROM INDIA

LET'S SEE WHO CAN LIFT THIS STONE.

THE KLING WARRIOR COULD NOT LIFT THE STONE...

BUT WHEN BADANG LIFTED THE ROCK...

IT LANDED AT THE MOUTH OF THE SINGAPORE RIVER,

WHERE IT STOOD FOR CENTURIES.

IT WAS DISCOVERED IN 1819 BY LABOURERS CLEARING THE JUNGLE.

IT BECAME KNOWN AS THE SINGAPORE STONE.

UNFORTUNATELY, THE STONE WAS BLOWN UP IN 1843 WHEN THEY WIDENED THE RIVER.

SOME FRAGMENTS WERE SAID TO HAVE BEEN SENT TO CALCUTTA MUSEUM, BUT THEIR WHEREABOUTS IS UNKNOWN. THE ONLY KNOWN PIECE CAN BE SEEN AT THE NATIONAL MUSEUM OF SINGAPORE. THE STONE CONTAINS 50 LINES OF SCRIPT THAT ARE BELIEVED TO HOLD SECRETS TO SINGAPORE'S ANCIENT PAST. BUT TILL NOW, NO ONE CAN DECIPHER THEIR MEANING.

OH, A PUZZLE!

BLESSINGS FROM THE SWORDFISH HEAD ROCK

THERE WAS ANOTHER STONE NEARBY, CALLED THE SWORDFISH HEAD ROCK.

THE SWORDFISH SKIMS ALONG THE SURFACE OF THE WATER, WITH ITS SNOUT STICKING OUT OF THE WATER. THEY ARE STRONG POWERFUL JUMPERS AND OFTEN LEAP OUT OF THE WATER.

THEY GET EXCITED BY THE LIGHT FROM THE BOATS AT NIGHT.

FISHERMEN HAVE BEEN "ATTACKED" BY SCHOOLS OF SUDDENLY EXCITED FISH.

SOMETIMES THEIR SHARP BEAKS BREAK OFF IN THE BODIES OF THE SAILORS! THESE FISH POSE AN EVEN GREATER DANGER THAN SHARKS!

THE ORANG LAUT, THE PEOPLE WHO LIVED IN THE AREA, BELIEVED THE ROCK CONTAINED SPIRITS. THEY BROUGHT OFFERINGS EVERY DAY. THEY WERE AFRAID IF THEY DID NOT, THE ROCK WOULD GET ANGRY AND BRING MISFORTUNE WHILE THEY WERE OUT AT SEA.

OH, A CURSE!

THE STORY OF SANG NILA UTAMA, AND HOW HE GAVE UP A CROWN FOR AN ISLAND

LONG AGO, IN PALEMBANG (MODERN DAY INDONESIA), THERE LIVED A PRINCE CALLED SANG NILA UTAMA.

ONE DAY, HE WENT HUNTING.

HE CHASED THE STAG TO THE TOP OF A HILL. HE SAW A BEAUTIFUL ISLAND ACROSS THE WATERS.

WHAT IS THAT ISLAND?

TEMASEK.

I MUST GO THERE.

SUDDENLY, A STORM APPEARED.

THEY THREW EVERYTHING OVERBOARD. BUT THE STORM DID NOT CALM DOWN.

THE ONLY THING THAT REMAINED WAS HIS CROWN.

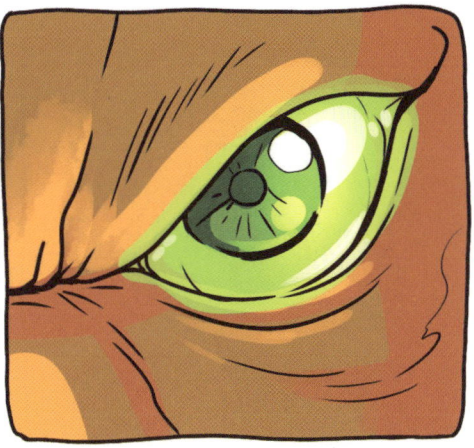

WHAT IS THE NAME OF THAT ANIMAL?

WE HAVE HEARD IN ANCIENT TIMES OF SUCH AN ANIMAL CALLED A SINGHA*.

THIS IS A FINE PLACE THAT CONTAINS SO FIERCE AND POWERFUL AN ANIMAL!

*SANSKRIT FOR "LION"

I NAME THIS ISLAND SINGAPURA*.

THUS, SANG NILA UTAMA SETTLED HERE, NAMED IT SINGAPURA, AND REIGNED OVER IT FOR 48 YEARS.

*LION CITY

IS THAT WHY WE HAVE THE MERLION?

YES, IT HAS THE BODY OF A FISH TO REMEMBER OUR BEGINNINGS AS A FISHING VILLAGE AND THE HEAD OF A LION TO GUARD THE RIVER.

A GUARDIAN ANGEL! I MEAN, A GUARDIAN LION!

BUT, GRANDPA, THERE ARE NO LIONS IN SINGAPORE.

OH, A MYSTERY!

THE ORANG LAUT WHO WERE HERE WHEN RAFFLES ARRIVED

THE EARLIEST PEOPLE WHO LIVED AROUND THE RIVER MOUTH WERE THE ORANG LAUT, OR "SEA PEOPLE".

THE ORANG LAUT SPENT A LARGE PART OF THEIR LIVES IN THEIR BOATS. THEY FISHED IN THE RIVERS, HUNTED IN THE MANGROVES AND MADE THEIR LIVING FROM HARVESTING THE TREASURES OF THE SEA.

THEY PLAYED AN IMPORTANT ROLE IN THE REGION. THEY WERE FAMILIAR WITH THE ROCKS AND CURRENTS OF THE AREA, AND OFTEN GUIDED TRADING SHIPS TO SAFETY.

THEY WERE ALSO FEARSOME SEA WARRIORS WHO HELPED TO GUARD THE WATERS OF THE REGION.

THE ORANG LAUT MUST HAVE BEEN SURPRISED TO SEE STAMFORD RAFFLES AND HIS MEN WHEN THEY LANDED NEAR THEIR SETTLEMENT AT THE MOUTH OF THE RIVER IN 1819.

THE SETTLEMENT WAS THEN GOVERNED BY TEMENGGONG* FOR THE SULTAN. THERE WERE ABOUT A THOUSAND ORANG LAUT LIVING THERE THEN.

Ships Boats
South Point
Treaty Tent
Cannon
Banqueting Tent
Red Carpet
TEMENGGONG'S HOUSE
ORANG LAUT
Singapore River
KAMPONG TEMENGGONG
Malay Boats

* HEAD OF SECURITY

A FEW DAYS LATER, RAFFLES SIGNED A TREATY WITH SULTAN HUSSEIN AND THE TEMENGGONG, AND SINGAPORE BECAME A BRITISH TRADING PORT. THIS DATE IS RECOGNISED AS THE FOUNDING OF MODERN SINGAPORE.

THE UNPOPULAR FORT FULLERTON

TO PROTECT THE HARBOUR AND WAREHOUSES, IN 1829, THE BRITISH BUILT A FORT AT THE MOUTH OF THE RIVER.

NOT EVERYONE WAS HAPPY WITH THE LOCATION OF FORT FULLERTON. THEY FELT IT WAS A WASTE OF A GREAT LOCATION, WITH GREAT VIEWS OF THE SEA.

THE CONSTANT ARTILLERY PRACTICE AFFECTED THE GODOWNS, SOMETIMES EVEN BRINGING DOWN THEIR ROOFS. ALSO, THE MERCHANTS WERE FEARFUL IT WOULD DRAW ENEMY FIRE RIGHT INTO TOWN.

FORT FULLERTON WAS DEMOLISHED IN 1873.

TODAY, THE FULLERTON HOTEL STANDS IN ITS PLACE.

OH, IT WAS UNPOPULAR!

WHEN RATS AND CENTIPEDES AND TOADS TERRORISED THE LAND

IN THE EARLY DAYS OF SETTING UP THE PORT, THERE WAS A PLAGUE OF RATS. THE RATS WERE AS BIG AS CATS!

OFFICIALS OFFERED A REWARD TO ANYONE WHO BROUGHT IN A RAT.

$$$

THE LOCALS BROUGHT THEM IN IN THE HUNDREDS!

THERE WERE SO MANY RATS THAT THEY HAD TO DIG A VERY DEEP PIT TO BURY THEM!

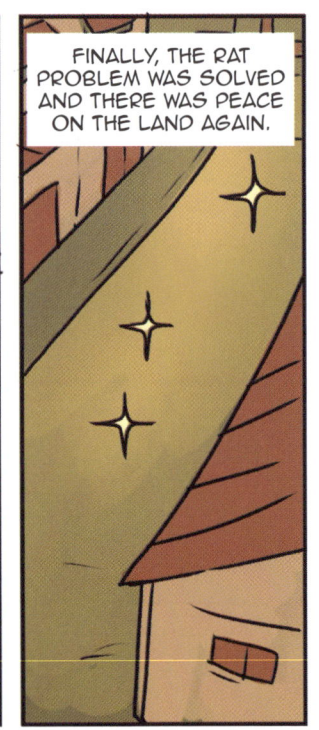

FINALLY, THE RAT PROBLEM WAS SOLVED AND THERE WAS PEACE ON THE LAND AGAIN.

SOME TIME LATER, A GREAT NUMBER OF CENTIPEDES APPEARED!

AGAIN, THEY WERE A NUISANCE TO THE PEOPLE LIVING BY THE RIVER. AGAIN, A REWARD WAS OFFERED.

SOON TOO, THE NUMBER OF CENTIPEDES STARTED TO DECREASE AND THE PEOPLE NO LONGER CRIED OUT IN PAIN FROM BEING BITTEN.

LATER, THERE WAS AN INFESTATION OF TOADS. SOME DID NOT MIND BECAUSE TOADS GOT RID OF MOSQUITOES, WHICH WAS ALSO A HUGE PROBLEM, BUT OTHERS DID NOT LIKE BEING KEPT UP AT NIGHT BY THEIR CROAKING.

AGAIN, A REWARD FOR EACH TOAD WAS OFFERED. AGAIN, THE LOCALS BROUGHT THEM IN DAILY AND SOON, THERE WAS RELATIVE QUIET AGAIN.

WOW, IT WAS A VERY... INSECT-Y AND PESTY PLACE!

CHAPTER 13 A LOST ISLAND

I HAVE ONE VERY SPECIAL STORY.

HOW WOULD YOU LIKE TO VISIT A LOST ISLAND?

LOST?

I USED TO GO THERE WHEN I WAS A BOY.

A LOST ISLAND... HOW COOL. YOU HAD ALL THE FUN, GRANDPA!

WELCOME TO PULAU SAIGON. SOME SAY IT WAS NAMED SO BECAUSE GOODS FROM SAIGON (VIETNAM) WERE STORED HERE.

ROBERTSON QUAY

FOOT BRIDGE

SINGAPORE RIVER

CLEMENCEAU
AVENUE BRIDGE

PULAU SAIGON

PULAU SAIGON ROAD

MAGAZINE ROAD

HAVELOCK ROAD

WHAT IS THAT SMELL?

BESIDES WAREHOUSES, THERE WAS ALSO THE CITY'S RUBBISH INCINERATOR. PIGS WERE ALSO BROUGHT HERE TO BE... WELL, PROCESSED AT THE ABATTOIR. THE BRIDGE WE CAME ACROSS WAS ALSO CALLED BUTCHER BRIDGE.

SNIFF

THERE'S ANOTHER SMELL. A NICE ONE. LIKE PEPPER AND HERBAL SOUP.

I RECOGNISE IT. IT SMELLS LIKE... LIKE... BAK KUT TEH!

SOME SAY THIS WAS THE ORIGINAL HOME OF BAK KUT TEH.

HOW COME I ONLY GOT BONES?

THAT'S WHAT BAK KUT TEH USED TO BE LIKE. 'KUT' MEANS BONES.

THE COOLIES COULD NOT AFFORD TO EAT MEAT. THE ABBATOIR WAS A CHEAP SOURCE OF BONES.

THEY BOILED THE BONES WITH CHINESE HERBS TO MAKE BONE SOUP.

THEY ALSO SAY THEY PICKED PEPPERCORN THAT FELL OUT OF THE SACKS THEY WERE CARRYING.

I'M GLAD NOWADAYS WE CAN AFFORD TO EAT BAK KUT TEH WITH MEAT ON IT.

CHAPTER 14 THE RIVER OF LIFE

151

LET'S GO OUT WITH THE BUMBOAT AGAIN, GRANDPA.

The River continued to be the centre of trade, the lifeblood of the nation. Over time, as the volume grew too much to handle, and with the development of technology, trading activity moved to Keppel Harbour and will, in the future, move to Tuas Mega Port.

1977 marked a close to this chapter of the River's life. The government started to clean up the River. Bumboats which had plied the River for over 150 years, and squatters who had made their homes along the River, were resettled. The clean-up would take many years.

In 1984, 400 people jumped into the River for a mass swim, signalling a new chapter in its life.

Bibilography

My thanks to so many who had written and captured so much of life as it was on the River:

2022. [online] Available at: <https://www.roots.gov.sg/stories-landing/stories/the-singapore-river-story/story> [Accessed 2 May 2022].

Auger, T. (2015). *A river transformed: Singapore River and Marina Bay.* Urban Redevelopment Authority.

Berry, L. (1984). *Singapore's river: A living legacy.* Eastern Universities Press.

Biblioasia.nlb.gov.sg. 2022. A Beastly Business: Regulating the Wildlife Trade in Colonial Singapore. [online] Available at: <https://biblioasia.nlb.gov.sg/vol-17/issue-1/apr-jun-2021/beastly-business> [Accessed 2 May 2022].

Chew, M. (2001). *Memories of the Fullerton.*

Choo, F. (2016, January 19). *5 Interesting Facts About The Singapore River Clean-up.* The Straits Times. Retrieved May 5, 2022, from https://www.straitstimes.com/singapore/5-interesting-facts-about-the-singapore-river-clean-up

Cornelius, V., 2022. *Singapore River (historical overview) | Infopedia.* [online] Eresources.nlb.gov.sg. Available at: <https://eresources.nlb.gov.sg/infopedia/articles/SIP_148_2005-02-02.html> [Accessed 2 May 2022].

Cornelius, V., 2022. *Cavenagh Bridge | Infopedia.* [online] Eresources.nlb.gov.sg. Available at: <https://eresources.nlb.gov.sg/infopedia/articles/SIP_2_2004-12-17.html> [Accessed 2 May 2022].

Diagana, M., & Angresh, J. (2014). F*ort Canning Park: Exploring Singapore's heritage.* ORO editions.

Dobbs, S. (2016). *The Singapore River: A Social History, 1819-2002.* NUS Press.

Eresources.nlb.gov.sg. 2022. *Orang laut | Infopedia.* [online] Available at: <https://eresources.nlb.gov.sg/infopedia/articles/SIP_551_2005-01-09.html> [Accessed 2 May 2022].

Frost, M. R., & Balasingamchow, Y.-M. (2013). *Singapore: A Biography.* Didier Millet.

Hon, J. (1990). *Tidal fortunes: A story of change: The Singapore river and Kallang Basin.* Landmark Books.

Tony Boey at https://johorkaki.blogspot.com/ for many informative and interesting posts.

Koh, J., 2022. *Fort Fullerton | Infopedia.* [online] Eresources.nlb.gov.sg. Available at: [Accessed 2 May 2022]. Kwa, C. G. (2019). Seven Hundred Years: A history of Singapore. National Library Board.

Lee, Kok Leong (2019, December 20). R*iver of life — we & Singapore.* 从夜暮到黎明 *From dusk to dawn.* Retrieved May 5, 2022, from http://navalants. blogspot.com/2019/12/river-of-life-we-singapore.html

Pearson, Harold Frank. (1954). *Stories of Early Singapore.* University of London Press.

Malayannals.blogspot.com. (2022). *Variants.* [online] Available at: [Accessed 2 May 2022]. Miksic, J. N. (2014). Singapore & the silk road of the sea, 1300-1800. NUS Press.

Lee, Kok Leong (2021, September 17). *Singapore 100+ year old wooden boats and beyond.* 从夜暮到黎明 *From dusk to dawn.* Retrieved May 19, 2022, from https://navalants.blogspot.com/2021/09/singapore-100-year-old-wooden-boats-and.html

Tan, B. L., Chua, C. H., & Tanzer, M. (1986). *Singapore Lifeline: The river and its people.* Times Books International.

Tyers, R. K. (2018). *Singapore then and now.* Landmark Books. Yap, C. (1990). A Port's story.

Wise, Michael. Traveller's Tales of Old Singapore. Marshall Cavendish Editions, 2018.

Yip Yew Chong
http://yipc.com/blog/2020/07/pulau-saigon/

About the Author

Tina Sim likes to write about what life used to be like when her father was a boy — when the River was bustling with people, activities, sounds and smells too! He would have swum holding on to the back tyres of the bumboats as they pulled out at sea, or sat on the banks marvelling at the strength and agility of the coolies as they unloaded the heavy cargo. He would have enjoyed re-visiting River with her. These are as much her stories as his.

About the Artist

Alan Bay is an comic artist and illustrator who enjoys spreading happiness through his drawings. He likes to keep the spirit of childhood alive by drawing big monsters, magical dragons and pesky kids. His latest works include *The Intertidal Adventures of Biogirl MJ*, *Once Upon a Singapore... Traders* and *Guss' Gutsy Adventures*.

Our Thanks

To so many who have shared their stories with us — in books, via stories and images. Special thanks to Lee Kok Leong who generously looked through the early drafts to help us recreate the Singapore River of the past. Also to our early readers, Lauren Koh, Jyotsna Mishra, Low Jia En, Rene Lai, Isaac and Nathan Quah for giving us invaluable inputs in our early drafts. And to you, our readers, we hope you enjoy reading this book as much as we enjoyed writing it for you.